T0370482

The Art of Nothing
My Path to Inner Peace and Love

Beatrice Pitocco

AuthorHouse™
1663 Liberty Drive
Bloomington, IN 47403
www.authorhouse.com
Phone: 1 (800) 839-8640

Published by AuthorHouse 03/04/2016

ISBN: 978-1-5049-8382-2 (sc)
ISBN: 978-1-5049-8383-9 (e)

Library of Congress Control Number: 2016903551

The Art of Nothing

My Path to Inner Peace and Love

Simple, self-reflective thoughts on achieving inner peace and love.

By: Beatrice Pitocco

The Buddhists believe that the First Noble Truth is suffering. To live is to suffer, or so they say.

In my efforts to try and understand this life, I have realized that life is nothing more than a dream. We all have to suffer something in this lifetime, and in doing so, we have a choice in the way we accept our very own suffering.

There isn't a soul on this planet that has not had to suffer something, be it illness, loss, hardship of some kind, war, destruction, or loneliness.

In my own quest to find my own inner peace, I have taken to the Art of Nothing. I have stopped searching to fill the void, and in contrast have tried, as best I could to come to terms with the loneliness that has been the only thing that never seems to leave me alone.

To live is to suffer. How you suffer is a choice. Choose well. – Beatrice

Dedication:

I dedicate this book to every single person who has ever existed in my life; the main characters, and also the passerby's. The faces I pass every day without thinking twice who make up the scenery of my silly little life. I dedicate this book to the people who have hurt me, intentionally or not, because only pain allows us to grow. I dedicate this to the select few, who know me, truly know me and love me. I love you more.

Life is Illusion. What you see isn't necessarily what is true. Mirror images, mixed signals, misunderstanding. The truth is, there is no truth other than that which you believe. And everyone has their own truth.

Every soul has a truth inside of them that may never be known, including you. The key is to learn your truth, live by it, and reserve judgment on the truth of others.

Life is illusion. Life is a dream.

If you can remember that life is nothing more than a dream, you may choose not to take things so seriously. After all, everyone's life really can be described in much the same way; a comedic tragedy of sorts, where nothing makes sense, and more often than not, nothing ever will.

Montreal, Quebec

Toronto, Ontario

Don't look back. It is difficult not to look back at times, but life moves forward, not backward.

Seek out new adventures, learn to be alone. The most difficult relationship we will ever have is with our own selves.

Look forward. Never look back.

Find yourself. Find yourself in the most unusual of spaces. Find yourself when you aren't looking, in the quietness of the morning while the world is asleep. As your eyes open to face a new dawn; it is precisely then, that you will find yourself.

Find yourself when there isn't anyone to please, nothing to hide from; as you unabashedly recount all of your triumphs and your deepest scars. Slowly move your hand along the scars that life has so helplessly handed you;

And without so much as a warning, *you will find yourself.*

Edmonton, Alberta

Halifax, Nova Scotia

Understand that there is an invisible fine line, between joy and pain. Most of us live in the deep crevasse of that fine line our entire lives, not knowing how to leave that place.

I have never seemed to mind, or ever wanted to leave that place. There is something so magical about seeing both sides of the coin at once. There is something so haunting about being in the in-between. For every tear, laughter is around the corner and in every joyous moment, a pang of sadness always seems imminent.

Learn to love the melancholy of it all. In some ways, ***it is the most honest thing you will ever feel.***

Learn to find comfort in strangers.

It seems easier to love people you don't know. I've never really understood this. But I know that I will never be truly alone as long as I am a stranger to someone.

Sudbury, Ontario

Emeryville, California

Solitude is haunting. Like an empty street, it can be frightening. It is said that loneliness is God's way of calling to us. When we are busy, with life, with people, with plans and things, rarely do we seek His grace.

But alone, in the catacombs of our thoughts, and mind, we yearn. We yearn to love and to be loved. We yearn to have a simple hand to hold. We recognize our own frailty, and wonder about the purpose and meaning, if ever there was one.

And it is in those moments, when you are closest to God.

Do not fear solitude; do not fear yourself. You are your own worst enemy. Trust that everything in your life is perfect, regardless of how imperfect it may seem. And in that knowledge, find your peace.

Everyone is broken. In one way or another, we are all so very broken. We spend an eternity trying to somehow fix ourselves, and yet, there is beauty in the brokenness. The light shines through the cracks. Being broken doesn't mean there is anything wrong with you. On the contrary, any difficulty you face offers an opportunity to have greater empathy for others. It is a choice, your choice really, to play victim or to save yourself. And you are not alone. The Universe, in all its magnificence, is waiting, with baited breath, for you to realize just how much light can shine through you.

Don't fix yourself.

Forgive yourself.

And be proud of who you are. For all your brokenness, you are eternally whole.

Scugog, *Ontario*

Our Lady of Victory Basilica, *Buffalo, New York*

You are not alone.

Never feel that you are alone in this life. For all it's wickedness, there is beauty everywhere. There are angels, who guide you, if you believe. Have faith, especially when it is most difficult. It is in your most difficult moments, when your angels are the saddest. And when all else fails, and everyone leaves, know, with all your knowing, your angels won't rest until you do.

The Art of Nothing.

If you try to be good you defeat the purpose. If you search for truth, for God, they elude you. To understand, you must first be utterly confused. To become aware is to transcend continually your thought. It is to stop trying to control anyone, anything, any outcome and just be. The Art of Nothing. To see others and love others for who they are, truly, you must first love yourself and accept yourself completely.

Stop trying. Let go. Be grateful.

Be kind. Be honest.

The first step in attaining peace is to stop trying to find it. Peace, much like love, much like God, are never found, for they were never lost. When you are ready, they find you.

Emeryville, California

Peggy's Cove, *Nova Scotia*

Be a beacon of light.

Every day you wake up, you have a choice to make. Will you be someone's light or will you be their darkness?

Be a beacon of light, whenever you can. In lighting someone else's path, your own path will shine bright. It isn't always easy to find the strength, to shine. And in those moments when you simply can not, know, that someone else will bring light to you. And so it goes, this dance we call life. Enjoy it, while you can, when you can. Life is nothing more than a tragic comedy, an illusion, a dream.

And therefore, to anyone reading: Sweet Dreams.

Do not get too caught up in this world.

If you become too attached to this world, you risk getting lost.

We can easily become spiritually lost, amidst the bright
lights, noisy confusion, beautiful people, lustful desires.

But do not get too caught up in this world. This is not it.
Whatever you seek you will not find outside of the walls
of your own inner being. Remember this. Especially when
your soul feels as though it is being pulled in a direction
you know, instinctively is not correct. Listen to your inner
voice, your intuition is your soul's whisper, in your moments
of great decisions. You will know when you feel out of sync.
Often it is when you are too caught up, in this world.

Vancouver, British Columbia

San Francisco Airport

Look at your surroundings. Be amazed at what human beings can create when they are inspired. See everything around you, and be truly in awe; for man-made structures are often wrought with unimaginable creativity.

Be inspired by your fellow man, to achieve more than what you think you can. As a human you have unlimited potential. Believe that you can do great things.

For if you do not believe in yourself, no one will.

Nothing is ever what it seems.

Nothing is ever truly black or white. Do not hold too firmly your own ideas of what life should be.

It is not your job to determine right from wrong for anyone other than your own self.

We all have a path, filled with many different colors. Do not become so rigid in your beliefs that you are unable to admire the vast differences that exist in this world. For it is our differences, that make us the same. Once you understand this, you will understand.

Papagayo, Costa Rica

Venice, Italy

Travel.

Travel, when you can, wherever you can; even if that means
simply getting lost in your very own city or town.

Travel, not to boast, or to become worldly. Many
small minds have traveled far around the globe,
and yet their minds have remained closed.

Rather, travel to recognize, that no matter where you
go, there is no distinction between the human race.

We are all the same, on the inside. The faster you
understand this, the more empathy you will have, giving
you a sense of freedom, and a detachment from all the
people, places and things that this very limited world
can offer, regardless of how beautiful they may be.

Some people can only show the level of respect, honesty, truth and kindness they reserve for themselves.

Don't be angry with them.

Instead, pray for them. Their struggle is more difficult than you can imagine. People are never against you. They are just for themselves before anyone else. Their struggle is on the inside, just like yours. So pray for them, and let it go.

Edmonton, Alberta

Dubai, United Arab Emirates

There is no difference between life and
death. The two are interchangeable.

This existence is death in the same way it is life.

There is no difference. I have seen many men who are
dead on the inside, but walk amongst the living.

And I know many dead souls whose memory is still
very much alive. This journey is one of discovery -

Discover what you can, and be less worried about life and
death. They are both equally joyful, and painful in due course

Time is limited. We are not bound to anything or anyone, contrary to our own desires and beliefs.

Enjoy who and what is in your life, when you have it. Take nothing for granted. And learn the art of letting go, surrendering to what is not meant for you.

If you trust the Universe, know this:

What is meant for you, will always find it's way to you. Trust that everything, absolutely everything, in your life is as it should be.

Bari Vecchia, Italy

Ocho Rios, Jamaica

If you fear your own self, you will never find peace. The truth we seek is not here, except for our own inner truth.

Be true to you, whoever you are.

Being true to yourself, will allow you the grace to find your peace. The most difficult challenge in life is understanding who you are; the second most difficult challenge is being true to who that is, and not being afraid of your very own self.

Try not to get too attached to anything in this world. We are momentary glimpses of the future to those who came before, and momentary glimpses of the past to those who come after. We are temporary, and so is everything else. The only indelible mark you can leave this world with, is the love that you share, and how you chose to treat yourself and others.

Love yourself, love others, be kind, but try not to get too attached to anything in this very limited world.

Highway 401, St. Catharines, Ontario

Polignano a Mare, Italy

I believe that the longer we live, the less we truly know. Life seems to be a mixture of choice and chance, highs and lows that somehow intertwine to assimilate some sort of storyline. Everyone becomes a part of everyone else's plot, sometimes as a main character and sometimes as a passerby.

None of this makes any sense, but perhaps it isn't supposed to. Human existence is a complex contradiction of good and bad, right and wrong, a constant changing, a constant evolution.

Perhaps then, the point is to transcend. To transcend the conundrum of trying to find a purpose, and instead, live the life we have purposefully.

To transcend is to become aware. To become aware is to wake up. To wake up, is to be alive.

Until then, you are only asleep.

Open your eyes.

Do not miss the beauty that surrounds you by seeking what is not there. Try, with all your might, to see the world that is around you now. There is no such thing as the next best thing. If you can not appreciate what you have, you will never be satisfied with anything more. Attention, is the purest form of intimacy.

Trust me on that

Vatican City

Ocho Rios, Jamaica

Love and attraction are more often than not based on projection. As such, love, as we know it, is more conditional than not. And yet love can allow us to see ourselves, our own faults, if we are aware, through our interactions with others, and through our own understanding of the concept of love.

We rarely see others as they are – more so, we see them as we are.

Our lovers, our partners, our friends, and those closest to us, are often a mirror or conduit, an opportunity to see other parts of ourselves, through them.

So love with all your heart, but try your best, not to become too attached, or lose yourself, in the state of 'love'. Nothing lasts forever, nothing ever should.

Do not become unhinged. People may say or do things that hurt you. Do not get angry, do not harbor resentment and most importantly, do not let other people's thoughts or idea's about who you are, derail your emotional stability.

Most people barely know themselves, so then, how can they know you?

Forgive people, and understand that hurt people, *hurt people.* Very few people will be truly interested in what you have to say. If you find someone who is, cherish them. People like that are hard to find.

Toronto, Ontario

Emeryville, California

Never be afraid to say what you feel. What you feel is usually the most authentic part of you that exists, and in a world so full of trickery and treachery, never be afraid to display any authenticity you can. The world needs it; you need it.

Don't be afraid of what you feel.

If you love someone, tell them - even if they don't love you back. Saying what you feel may hurt at first, but it will free you in ways you can't imagine. Only something that is fake can ever be foolish. Something that is false has always the possibility of being found out as nothing more than a forgery.

But what you feel is truth, is authentic, is the real thing. Don't fear it - embrace it and gift it to the world. Liberty and freedom come from truth. That is undeniable

Do something out of the ordinary, surprise someone. As we get older, we recognize with intense vigor, the beauty of simplicity.

**Write a letter, phone a friend, buy someone
a gift for absolutely no reason.**

It is the simple things in life, we end up
missing the most. Never forget that.

San Francisco Airport

Papagayo, Costa Rica

Don't look for someone to be the love of your life.

Be the love of someone else's life.

Give the love you wish to receive. If you can achieve this level of selflessness, it is guaranteed that love, will flow to you, and through you, like waves hitting the shore.

Love isn't about what you want someone to do for you.

Love is doing for others, and if you understand this, the Universe will always reward you with love, when you least expect it, and need it the most.

A Requiem, by definition, is a service, or mass celebrated for the repose of the souls of the dead.

Do not wait until death for your Requiem, for your repose. Do not wait for death to celebrate your soul.

Become one with your soul, and learn to find peace and tranquility now.

For it is better to find peace amongst the living, than amongst the dead.

Montreal, Quebec

Peggy's Cove, *Nova Scotia*

It is a wise person, who understands the value of humility.

No matter how big, wealthy or powerful you feel you are, in the grandness of it all, you are smaller than a grain of sand on the beach. Never forget your place in this world. You may find yourself on top today, but winds change and wheels turn. Be grateful, and humble, especially when you are winning. We are all great in our own ways, and yet the most ordinary thought in the world, is to think of yourself as special or unique.

Never fear growing, even if growth means leaving your comfort zone, and standing alone, in the midst of sameness.

This life is meant for you to discover, evolve and learn about truth - whatever that means to you.

And on your journey you may sometimes stand alone. In those times, stand strong, like a tree in a field of flowers.

And grow high so that you may offer shade to those below.

Uxbridge, Ontario

Polignano a Mare, Italy

Do not underestimate the power of freedom.

If ever you find yourself alone, cherish the aloneness. Rarely will you find yourself so free. Freedom, comes from radically accepting your own loneliness, and embracing the beauty of being at one with you.

Cherish all stages of your life, even the painful ones.

They all have their lessons.

They all have their seasons.

They all have their endings.

They all have their reasons.

The same magnificence, who created the breathtaking mountains, created you. Never forget this.

You were created in the same glory, as the stars and the moon, the sun and the sky. Your beauty is uniquely yours - cherish it. Your beauty has little to do with your physicality, so do not become too consumed with outer beauty.

Although the mountains are beautiful to look at, it is their strength, and the beauty you can not see, that renders them magnificent.

The same applies to you. Your beauty, lies in what the eyes can not see but what the heart can feel.

Jasper, Alberta

Montreal, Quebec

Frida Kahlo said it best:

'I hope the exit is joyful,

and I hope never to return'

I believe there is a world, outside of this one,
that has the answers, I have been seeking my
entire life, but of which, I may never find.

If this other world exists, I hope that I go there,
when my stay on this planet is complete.

I hope wherever we go, it is a place, where love,
in its' purest form, is the dominant force.

Because the only truth I have ever known,
resides in pure, authentic love.